DATE DUE

THINK ABOUT

Being in a
WHEELCHAIR

Lois Keith

Smart Apple Media

First published in the UK in 1998 by

Belitha Press Limited
London House, Great Eastern Wharf,
Parkgate Road, London SW11 4NQ

Text and illustrations copyright © Belitha Press Limited 1998
Cover design by Kathy Petelinsek

Published in the United States by
Smart Apple Media
123 South Broad Street
Mankato, Minnesota 56001

U.S. publication copyright © 2000 Smart Apple Media
International copyright reserved in all countries. No part of this book may be
reproduced in any form without written permission from the publisher.
Printed in Singapore

Library of Congress Cataloging-in-Publication Data

Keith, Lois.
Being in a wheelchair / Lois Keith.
p. cm. — (Think about)
Includes index.
Summary: Examines the challenges of being in a wheelchair, discussing why some people
cannot walk and how those who use a wheelchair function at school, at home, in sports,
and going to work.
ISBN 1-887068-87-2
1. Physically handicapped—Transportation—Juvenile literature.   2. Handicapped—
Orientation and mobility—Juvenile literature.   3. Wheelchairs—Juvenile literature.
[1. Wheelchairs.   2. Physically handicapped.]   I. Title.   II. Series: Think about
(Mankato, Minn.)

HV3022.K43   1999
362.4'3—dc21   98-39024

9 8 7 6 5 4 3 2 1

Photographs by: Allsport, Clive Brunskill, Todd Warshaw, Breckenridge & Viana, Collections,
Anthea Sieveking, Brian Shuel, Roger Scruton, Corbis-Bettman/UPI, Disability Now, John
Grooms Association, Louise Dyson Agency, Mary Evans Picture Library, Format Partners,
Brenda Price, Joanne O'Brien, Ulrike Preuss, Gisele Freund/Agence Nina Beskow, Getty
Images, Andrea Booher, Ken Fisher, Yaun Layma, Hugo Glendinning/CandoCo Dance
Company, Ronald Grant Archive, Warner Bros., Sally & Richard Greenhill, Robert Harding
Picture Library, Hulton Getty, Image Bank, L. D. Gordon, Long & Stebbens, London
Metropolitan Archive, Mattel UK Ltd, Motivation/David Constantine, Photofusion, David
Tothill, Pictor, Uniphoto, Quest Enabling Designs Ltd, Redferns, Leon Morris, Rex Features,
Sipa Press, Tim Rooke, Colin Schofield, Lord Mayor Treloar Archive, North Hampshire
Hospitals NHS Trust

Words in **bold** are explained in the glossary on pages 30 and 31.

ABOUT THE AUTHOR

Lois Keith, who uses a wheelchair, writes, teaches high school English, gives talks, and runs writing workshops. She also has written several award-winning books about disabilities.

Contents

People who use wheelchairs

There are many different reasons that people use wheelchairs. Some people can walk a little but use a wheelchair if they have a long way to go. Other people's legs don't work at all, so they have to use a wheelchair all the time. To many people with physical disabilities, it is their only way of getting around.

Look around you

Some places are more **accessible** to wheelchair-users than others. In a modern shopping mall, for example, where everything is on one level or where there are elevators available, there may be many people who use wheelchairs. But in places with uneven surfaces, stairs, or curbs without **ramps**, a person is less likely to see anyone using a wheelchair.

Sets of wheels

Choosing the right wheelchair is like buying a new pair of shoes; people need to find a pair that fits them just right. It is important for disabled people to use a wheelchair that is the right size for them. If the wheelchair is too big or too small, too heavy or too light, it will be much more difficult to use.

▶ Many big shopping malls now have elevators and escalators.

Types of wheelchairs

There are many types of wheelchairs. A chair that people push themselves by turning the wheels is called a manual wheelchair. Some people prefer motorized wheelchairs. These wheelchairs are strong and are operated by pushing a button on the arm of the chair. Motorized wheelchairs are powered by batteries. Other people have light wheelchairs that are easy to fold up and put in a car. This kind of wheelchair is used by many people who can walk a little.

Some people need help pushing their chair, but many people who use wheelchairs prefer to move the chair themselves even if they have someone with them.

This wheelchair is designed for children. The seat moves up or down so children can sit at the same table as their friends, reach high shelves, or pick things off the floor.

THINK ABOUT

Getting around

If you used a wheelchair, could you get into your home? Would you be able to go into your classroom at school or out onto the playground with your friends? Most people who use wheelchairs can get around very well where the pavement or the floor is flat and smooth. Staircases are difficult or impossible for wheelchair users, but elevators can help them go nearly anywhere other people go.

Why can't some people walk?

There are many reasons that people have difficulty walking. Some people are born with a condition that affects the way they move. Other people have an accident or get a disease as they are growing up or when they are older.

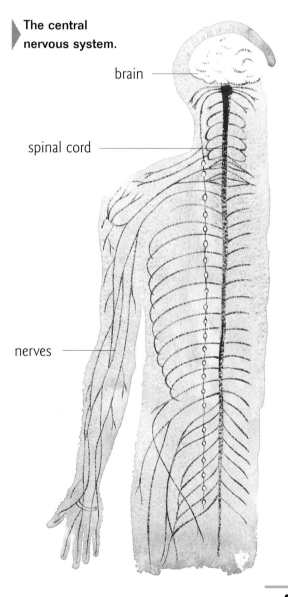

The central nervous system.

brain

spinal cord

nerves

The spinal cord

On the back of a person's neck are some hard knobs that stick out and run down the middle of the back. These bony segments are called **vertebrae**. They protect the **spinal cord**, which is soft and bendable. The spinal cord contains millions of **nerves** that send messages from the brain to all parts of the body. For example, if a person wants to move his toes, his brain sends the message through the spinal cord, along the nerves, down the legs to the feet. When the message reaches the muscles in the toes, they can move.

Damage to the spinal cord

A person's spinal cord can be damaged in an accident or by a condition such as **spina bifida** or **multiple sclerosis**. If this happens, commands from the brain can't reach other parts of the body. This means that many parts of the body become **paralyzed**.

Other wheelchair users

Some people who use wheelchairs have conditions—such as **muscular dystrophy** or **cerebral palsy**—that affect control of their muscles. Some people have a disease called **osteogenesis imperfecta** that makes their bones very brittle. Other people have **arthritis**.

These are just a few of the reasons that some people use wheelchairs. But whatever the reason, a wheelchair is not a prison for the disabled. It is an important piece of equipment that gives people the freedom to go where they want.

▲ Tanni Grey is a successful athlete. She was born with spina bifida and has used a wheelchair since she was seven. Tanni has won Paralympic gold medals for wheelchair racing and has won several major marathons.

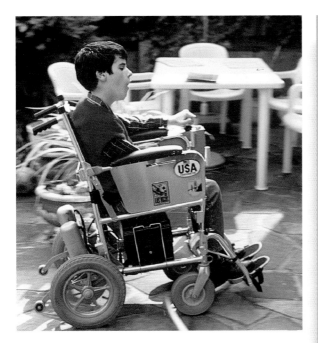

▲ This boy has cerebral palsy. People with this condition may have trouble using their arms or their legs.

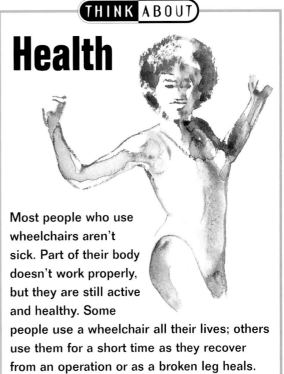

THINK ABOUT

Health

Most people who use wheelchairs aren't sick. Part of their body doesn't work properly, but they are still active and healthy. Some people use a wheelchair all their lives; others use them for a short time as they recover from an operation or as a broken leg heals.

A history of wheelchair users

Physical disabilities can affect people of all ages, forcing them to use a wheelchair. In the first half of the 20th century, many physically disabled people were younger than 14, but most people in wheelchairs today are older. This is because many childhood illnesses are easier to prevent today. Older people are more likely to need a wheelchair, because their bodies are not as strong as they used to be.

Poverty and disease

In the past, children often became disabled because they were poor. Children who lived in houses without proper toilets or clean water were sick or weak. They often caught diseases that prevented their bodies from growing properly. Children who did not have enough healthy food to eat often developed **rickets**, which made their legs thin and weak. Thousands of children in the first half of this century suffered from a disease called **polio**. Many of them died or became disabled. Doctors were expensive, so if a child became ill or had an accident, many parents could not afford medical treatment for them.

▷ **This photograph of poor Hungarian children was taken in 1920. The girl is suffering from rickets. Even today there are many parts of the world where children do not get enough healthy food or medical attention.**

Getting a wheelchair

Finding a good wheelchair was a problem for many people who couldn't walk. Wheelchairs were very expensive, and most families could not afford them. Poorer parents often made their own using scrap materials so that their disabled child could move around more.

▲ This wheelchair was sold in 1844.

Children in stories

Many famous children's books tell stories about disabled people who are magically cured. In the book *Heidi*, a disabled girl named Clara is suddenly able to walk, so she doesn't have to depend on other people any more. In the past, many people believed that wheelchair users could not be independent or active.

(THINK ABOUT)

Superstition

In the past, there was a lot of ignorance, fear, and superstition about disabled people, who were often labeled as cripples or physical defectives. Some people believed that having a disabled child was punishment for bad things the family had done, and that the child was possessed by evil spirits. Disabled children were very frightened by these attitudes. Things are better today, but sometimes disabled people are still presented in a negative way. Negative stereotypes can make people uncomfortable around those who use wheelchairs and can hurt the feelings of disabled people.

◀ This is a scene from a film called *The Secret Garden*. The story is about a boy named Colin who has spent most of his life in bed. He is furious when someone calls him a "poor crippled boy," so he pushes his wheelchair away and walks. In real life, there are few miraculous cures for people who cannot walk.

Schools of the past

In the first half of the 20th century, a lot of people feared the disabled and were **prejudiced** against them. Many disabled children did not go to school. Some teachers refused to teach them because they thought that the way disabled children looked might frighten the other students.

▶ If disabled children were sent to school at all, they often did not get a good education. The boys at this school had to make their own chairs to sit on.

Staying at home

Disabled children often had to stay at home instead of going to school. This was very upsetting for children who wanted to learn to read and write and to play with their friends. They would see their brothers and sisters going to school and would feel left out. Some disabled children went to elementary school but were not allowed to go on to high school. Parents tried to teach their children at home, but it wasn't the same. A few teachers did try to include disabled children in school life, but this did not happen very often.

Special schools

Some children who couldn't walk were sent to special schools. The children did some math and a little bit of reading, but they spent most of the time sewing or making simple crafts. Children who were sent to these schools were often bored and wished that they could go to ordinary schools. The separation in schools made them feel left out and different from other children.

Children of all ages at special schools were given the same simple lessons. Some people believed that children who couldn't walk would not be able to learn either.

Many people believed that plenty of fresh air would help to cure disabled children, so classes were often held outside.

Sent away to school

Children were sometimes as young as three years old when they were sent away to a special school. The school could be a long way from home, and sometimes parents were allowed to visit only once a year. Families who were very poor couldn't afford to visit at all. Special schools could be cruel places where children often had their hair cut short and wore numbered uniforms. If the teachers or nurses wanted to see a child, they called out a number instead of a name. Children in these schools often felt lonely and hopeless.

(THINK ABOUT)

Types of schools

Some people think that it is better for all children who use wheelchairs to go to school with other children who use wheelchairs. Other people believe that all children should be able to go to their local school with their friends, brothers, and sisters. What do you think?

Schools today

In recent years, many schools have made changes so that students in wheelchairs can move around easily. These changes may include wider door frames, special bathroom stalls, and ramps on the playground. These features allow all students to have equal access to all parts of the school.

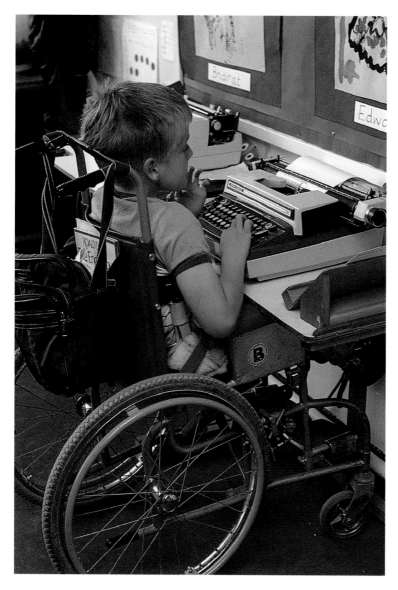

Designing a school

Some new schools are specially designed to include disabled students, including children who use wheelchairs. Many schools are on one floor only with smooth, even surfaces that are easier to wheel around on. There are also sometimes certain areas where people in wheelchairs can go if they need some special physical education classes.

Students who use wheelchairs can join in every school activity, although some things might need to be changed slightly. For example, the height of the tables could be adjusted so that wheelchair users could sit at them.

This classroom has an adjustable table. It has been set at just the right level for this boy.

School buildings

Some existing school buildings were built many decades ago. At that time, people did not think about including children who used wheelchairs, so many of these schools have lots of stairs. But everyone can be included if a few changes are made. Ramps can be used instead of a few stairs. Some schools have new classrooms added on to the ground floor, and other schools have an elevator installed.

▷ This school has a ramp alongside stairs to a classroom.

△ These boys enjoy playing soccer during recess at school.

Extra activities

It isn't too hard to include everyone in school activities. It just takes a little thought and planning. Many field trips from school may require extra planning if students in wheelchairs are to be included. When playing sports or other games during recess, the games may need to be adjusted so that everyone can play.

THINK ABOUT

On the playground

What games do you like to play on the playground? Could classmates in wheelchairs play too? You might have to change the game a bit to let them join in. Someone in a wheelchair could easily join in a game of tag. If your playground surface is smooth, they might move faster than you can run! If you lowered the basketball hoop, they could join in that kind of game as well.

At home

Moving around inside homes in a wheelchair can be a challenging experience. People who use wheelchairs like to have a lot of room to move around, so it is important that the house is kept clean and free of obstacles. Items left laying on the floor in the middle of the room, for example, can be frustrating for a person trying to move around in a wheelchair.

Around the house

People who use wheelchairs need to be able to get to all rooms. Apartments are usually on one level only, but there are ways to **adapt** a house that has stairs. Ramps can be built in places where there are just a few stairs, such as outside steps that lead to the front door.

This woman has had her front sidewalk specially designed so that it is a gentle slope instead of steps. This allows her to go in and out of her house easily. Slopes are also helpful for people pushing baby carriages, riding bicycles, or roller-skating.

The right height

It can be frustrating for anyone trying to reach items or shelves that are set at an inaccessible height. Height is a very important consideration to wheelchair users. For example, toilets for disabled people are often higher. In the kitchen, it is easier for someone in a wheelchair to cook and prepare food if the countertop and the oven are lower than usual. Electrical outlets should be positioned in the middle of the wall rather than near the floor.

Children who use wheelchairs can do the same things at home as everyone else, as long as everything is accessible.

This is a special elevator that can be used to move from one floor of a home to another.

Home equipment

Many ordinary things at home can be adapted for a wheelchair user. It is easier for someone in a wheelchair to find something in a sliding drawer than it is to have to reach into deep cupboards. There is also a lot of special equipment available for people who use wheelchairs. In the bathroom, some people use a fold-down shower seat so that they can move from their wheelchair into the shower.

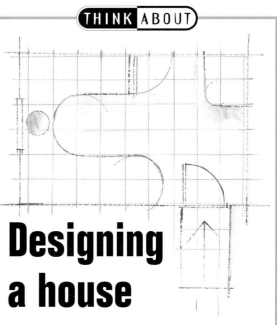

THINK ABOUT

Designing a house

Families include all sorts of people: children, older people, and people who are disabled. Architects are beginning to keep this in mind when they build new homes. For example, many new homes are now built with wider doors and hallways to help people in wheelchairs to move around. How would you design a new house so that someone who uses a wheelchair could live there?

Out and about

People who use wheelchairs like to go outside just like everyone else. It is important that there are flat surfaces to help them get around easily. Anything that has wheels will move along much easier if the path is smooth.

This mother has a baby seat attached to the front of her wheelchair. It helps her to go out with her children more easily.

Playgrounds

Many parks have playgrounds with swings, slides, and other fun equipment. Some disabled children can get out of their wheelchairs to play on the merry-go-round or jungle gym, but for others this is difficult. Some parks today have playground equipment that is redesigned so that children in wheelchairs can join in the fun.

(THINK ABOUT)

Helping people

Imagine that you are trying to lift a heavy box. It is nice if someone offers to help you carry it. But if you can handle the box yourself, it can be annoying if people pull the box out of your hands and carry it themselves. Sometimes people don't know whether they should ask disabled people if they would like help. When you think you could do something helpful for a person who uses a wheelchair, just ask him if he would like some help. If he doesn't need it, he will let you know.

Older buildings

In the past, disabled people were not expected to go outside much, so most older buildings were not designed to include wheelchair users. But by adding things such as ramps or elevators, buildings can be adapted so that everyone can use them.

Public transportation

It is often impossible for people who use wheelchairs to travel by bus, train, or subway. There are lots of steps and narrow doors to squeeze through. This makes many disabled people angry, because public transportation is often the only way to get around outside if they don't have a car.

A ramp makes this building accessible to wheelchair users.

Driving

Many adults who use wheelchairs drive their own car. They have special hand controls instead of foot pedals. Some disabled drivers fold up their wheelchair and put it in the car before driving off.

Some vans are adapted so that the driver can sit in his wheelchair. Other cars have a device that lifts the wheelchair onto the roof and stores it in a special compartment.

This van is adapted for wheelchair users. The driver wheels onto an elevator that rises to the van's floor. The driver moves behind the steering wheel, and the doors close by remote control.

Around the world

There may be as many as 20 million people around the world who need a wheelchair but can't afford one. Most of these people live in **developing countries**. Wheelchairs are expensive and hard to find in these parts of the world, which makes life very difficult for people who can't walk.

This man lost both his legs in a land mine explosion in Afghanistan. He uses a special three-wheeled chair and turns hand pedals to move the wheelchair forward.

Making wheelchairs

A charity called Motivation trains people in developing countries to design and build their own wheelchairs. The wheelchairs need to be simple and made with materials that local people can find easily.

The Motivation team has to think carefully about the design of different wheelchairs. In countries such as Cambodia, it is difficult to find the steel tubes usually used in wheelchairs, so the Motivation workers have designed a wheelchair made out of wood. In other countries such as Bangladesh, the roads can be very rough, so the wheelchairs need strong, extra-large wheels.

The right wheelchair

In poor countries, disabled children often have wheelchairs **donated** to them by richer countries. These wheelchairs are heavy, old, and much too big for children. Giving a child a wheelchair that is the wrong size is like giving her a huge pair of shoes and then telling her to run fast. Motivation makes wheelchairs that suit the age and needs of each person.

The Moti

A wheelchair has to last a long time in poor countries, so it is important that it can change as the child grows. Motivation has designed a chair for children called the Moti that is light, comfortable, and suits children of all ages and levels of disability. The Moti lets many children sit up, move around, and play for the first time.

These Indonesian men have been trained by the Motivation team to make wheelchairs.

This Russian boy has cerebral palsy. He was carried everywhere before he had a Moti wheelchair; now he can sit up and look around. The chair can be adjusted as he grows.

THINK ABOUT

Missing out

In some parts of the world, it is difficult or impossible to find wheelchairs for children who need them. These children have to stay home or lie in bed all day. If they have a condition such as cerebral palsy, their balance might not be good enough to sit up on their own. They need a good wheelchair so they can sit up and look around. Without a wheelchair, it is hard for these children to learn about the world around them.

Sports

Some people who use wheelchairs are very adventurous. They may go horseback riding, water-skiing, sailing, scuba diving, rappelling down cliffs, or even bungee jumping! Wheelchair users can take part in many sports. They might need help with some activities, but they can participate in many others on their own.

▶ Basketball is one event in the Paralympic Games. These Games take place at the same time as the Olympic Games. The Paralympics are for all disabled people, and there are many events for wheelchair athletes.

Basketball

Basketball is the most organized wheelchair sport. It has been played for more than 50 years. Wheelchair basketball started after World War II as an activity for fit young men who had been disabled during the war. The first teams had names such as the California Flying Wheels, Rolling Pioneers, and New Jersey Wheelers. Wheelchair basketball is now played by men and women all over the world. It is a fast-paced and exciting team game.

Skiing

With some special equipment and practice, people who use wheelchairs can even learn to ski. A skibob is a single ski with a lightweight, plastic seat attached for the skier to sit on. The skier uses his hands to help balance the skibob as he races downhill. Other people who are physically disabled use a special skiing sled with hand controls for steering.

A skibob competition in the Winter Paralympics.

Wheelchair racing

Many people in wheelchairs enjoy the challenge of racing in marathons. Wheelchairs built for racing are very lightweight and strong. Each chair is specially designed to fit one particular racer.

Wheelchair athletes train hard. They swim, work out in the gym, and can wheel more than 20 miles (32 km) a day.

THINK ABOUT

Your favorite sport

What kind of sports do you like? Do you like to play team games such as football or baseball, or do you prefer activities such as canoeing, rock climbing, or biking? Choose one activity and think of a way that a friend who uses a wheelchair could join in.

Fun and games

People who use wheelchairs like to have fun just like everyone else. Not everyone is athletic, but most disabled people would rather join in than watch. Whatever the activity—watching television, playing video games, fishing, reading, or shooting baskets— disabled children like to be involved too.

▷ This special lift makes getting into a swimming pool easy. The helper is turning a handle that lowers the swimmer into the water.

Swimming pools

Some community swimming pools have **facilities** for wheelchair users, but many others do not. Some disabled people can get to a swimming pool on their own, but once there they may need some help. Some pools have a special lift for disabled people. Wheelchair users move from their wheelchair into another seat that is lowered into the water. Many new pools have a gentle slope leading into the water instead of steps. Disabled people can borrow a special waterproof wheelchair and roll straight into the water.

All kinds of toys

Every child is different. Some are tall, and some are short; some are black, and some are white. Some like sports, while others prefer to paint. Some children walk, and others use wheelchairs. Today there are toys that reflect some of these differences.

The company that makes Barbie Dolls also makes a doll called Share a Smile Becky who uses a wheelchair. Unfortunately, the company didn't alter the Barbie house, so Becky couldn't get through her own front door.

Share a Smile Becky and typical Barbie Dolls.

Dance

Wheelchairs can move fast in many directions, and some people who use wheelchairs love to dance. CandoCo is a dance company with disabled and non-disabled dancers. The wheelchairs are part of the dance. They spin around, tip back, and are lifted into the air while the dancers motion with their arms.

The CandoCo dance group travels around the world to give performances and dance classes.

THINK ABOUT

Vacation

Everyone likes to go on vacation. Some people like relaxing vacations where they sit on the beach all day. Other people prefer active vacations. Campers and tents can be adapted for wheelchairs. This is great for children and adults who use wheelchairs and like active, outdoor vacations.

Going to work

Although disabled people have many talents and skills, it is not always easy for them to find work and show what they can do. Some people find it hard to believe that a disabled person can do a job as well as someone who is not disabled. Some employers are not willing to adapt their workplace so that someone in a wheelchair could get around. But when physically disabled people are given the chance, they can do an excellent job in many areas.

Working lives

World War II changed the working lives of many disabled people in the United States. As fit young men were called up into the army, navy, and air force, there was a desperate need for workers. Disabled people were given jobs in factories, hospitals, offices, and on farms. It was the first time that many disabled people had been able to work.

Today, many people in wheelchairs have jobs that they love doing and are very good at.

This woman is a model who has worked all over the world since 1994.

This man is a musician and television presenter who rappelled down a building as part of a campaign to make people aware of all the things that disabled people can do.

Jane's teachers never thought that she would have a job when she grew up. Now she works hard to make sure that disabled people are given equal rights at school and work.

Campaigning

Jane Campbell is a wheelchair user who **campaigns** for equal rights for disabled people. She runs an organization that helps disabled people to live independently in their own homes. Equal rights are very important to many disabled people like Jane. When she was young, she was sent to a special school with other children in wheelchairs. This meant that she was separated from her friends and missed out on the normal school experience.

THINK ABOUT

Careers

What kind of job would you like to have when you finish school? Maybe you're good at art and want to be an illustrator or designer, or maybe you'd like a glamorous job as a singer or actor. Perhaps you want to study to be a teacher, a doctor, or a lawyer. People who use wheelchairs can do all of these jobs.

Being a success

Some people think that wheelchair users sit around all day waiting for someone to come along and help them. Many people would be surprised if they knew how much people in wheelchairs can achieve. There have been many famous

wheelchair users throughout history. As attitudes change and disabled people are given the chance to prove what they can do, more and more people who use wheelchairs will be remembered for their talents and achievements.

Franklin D. Roosevelt hardly ever appeared in public in his wheelchair. Thousands of photographs of him were taken, but only two show him in a wheelchair. Here he is wearing braces to support his legs.

Franklin D. Roosevelt (1882-1945)

Franklin D. Roosevelt was the longest-serving American president, as well as one of the most admired. In 1921, he caught polio, which paralyzed his legs. Roosevelt was elected president in 1933. Many people thought that a disabled person couldn't do such an important job, but President Roosevelt helped to make the United States financially successful and led the country through World War II. He also set up an international center for the study and treatment of polio.

Frida Kahlo (1907-1954)

Frida Kahlo was a Mexican painter who married another famous artist named Diego Rivera. Kahlo loved to use bright colors in her paintings, many of which are self-portraits. She often wore traditional Mexican clothes with long skirts, shawls, and bright headdresses. When Kahlo was 18 years old, she was involved in a terrible accident and spent a lot of time in the hospital. Many of her paintings reflect her feelings about pain and illness.

▲ Frida Kahlo with her doctor. Her painting shows herself with a portrait of the doctor.

Itzhak Perlman (1945-)

Itzhak Perlman is a world-famous violinist. He was born in Israel and moved to the United States when he was 13 to study classical music. Perlman has made many recordings of his music and gives concerts all over the world. He had polio when he was young and now uses a wheelchair. Perlman is a strong believer in equal rights for disabled people.

▲ Stephen Hawking travels all over the world to give talks about his scientific theories.

◀ Itzhak Perlman playing in concert.

Stephen Hawking (1942-)

Stephen Hawking is a **physicist** and one of the most brilliant scientists of the 20th century. He is a professor at Cambridge University and has written many scientific books, the most famous of which is called *A Brief History of Time*. Hawking uses a wheelchair because he has a condition called **motor neuron disease**. This condition has also affected his voice, so he speaks through a computer.

THINK ABOUT

Finding out more

Try to find out more about the people on this page or about other famous people you've heard of who use wheelchairs.

Looking to the future

Most non-disabled people take it for granted that they can go to the bank, the mall, or the movies without worrying about getting into the buildings. Many times, people in wheelchairs find such places inaccessible to them. They might be told that they can't come in because the building has stairs or because it would be too dangerous. This is very upsetting to disabled people.

▲ All children should be given the chance to go to school with their friends.

Making improvements

All over the world, disabled people and their friends and families campaign to make sure that everyone has the same rights. Children who use wheelchairs should be able to go to the school where their brothers, sisters, and friends go if they choose to do so. Everyone should be able to get into public buildings such as libraries and theaters. They should be able to travel on buses and trains and should have the chance to go to college and to get good jobs.

Medical help

In the last 100 years, there have been many developments to help people who can't walk. There is now a **vaccine** to prevent polio, and **antibiotics** can cure many diseases. People who have lost arms or legs can get **artificial** ones that work almost as well as real limbs. Today there are operations to replace worn-out **joints** with metal ones.

What does the future hold?

Scientists are working to develop electrical devices that would help paralyzed muscles work by sending nerve impulses that would **bypass** damaged spinal cords. They are also trying to find cures for all kinds of crippling diseases. But many disabled people are less concerned about cures—which may be a long way off—than they are in having the same rights as everyone else.

▲ A mother who uses a wheelchair reads a book with her young daughter.

▲ A campaign to improve public transportation. In some cities, all buses have a platform that lowers to let wheelchair users roll straight onto the bus. This is also useful for parents with baby carriages.

THINK ABOUT

Equality

There will always be people who use wheelchairs. One hundred years ago, people who couldn't walk were often isolated and rarely went outside. If more buildings were designed with disabled people's concerns in mind, it would be a much fairer world for all people.

Glossary

accessible   Easy to enter or use. Buildings that are accessible to wheelchair users might have elevators or ramps and plenty of space inside.

adapted   Changed or improved. If a building is adapted for people who use wheelchairs, it might have wide doors and hallways.

antibiotic   A medicine that can cure diseases or stop them from becoming worse. An example of an antibiotic is penicillin.

arthritis   A painful condition in which joints become swollen and stiff. A person with arthritis in his leg joints may have difficulty walking.

artificial   Something that is man-made, not natural.

bypass   To go around or avoid. Devices are being developed that doctors hope will allow nerve messages to bypass the damaged spinal cords of people who are paralyzed.

campaign   To work to change something such as a law or attitude. People can campaign by giving speeches, writing books, letters, or articles, or organizing marches and demonstrations.

cerebral palsy   A disability that some people are born with or develop just after birth. People with cerebral palsy may have trouble using their arms and legs. Some might use a wheelchair and need help communicating.

developing countries
Poor countries that are trying to improve their farming, factories, and way of life.

donated   Given away, usually to a charity or to someone in need.

facilities   Equipment or an area designed to make things easier for people. One facility for people who use wheelchairs is a wide telephone booth with a telephone that is lower than usual.

joints   Places in the body where two bones are joined so that each bone can move freely. An example of a joint is the knee, which connects the bones in the leg.

motor neuron disease
A disease in which a person's motor nerves—the nerves that carry messages to muscles to make them move—stop working properly. This makes the muscles very weak.

multiple sclerosis   A disease of the brain, spinal cord, and nerves. Multiple sclerosis affects muscles and can sometimes paralyze limbs and affect a person's sight and speech.

muscular dystrophy
A disease that gradually destroys muscles, limiting a person's walking ability.

nerves   Tiny, thin connections that carry messages from the brain to all parts of the body.

paralyzed   A state in which a person cannot move or feel parts of his body. Damage to a person's brain, spinal cord, or nerves can result in paralysis.

osteogenesis imperfecta
A disease in which a person's bones crack or break very easily. It is sometimes referred to as "brittle bones disease."

physicist A person who studies physics, the scientific study of matter and energy.

polio An infectious disease often caught by children. If the infection reaches the spinal cord, it can damage muscles. Today, children are given a vaccine as babies to protect them from the disease. In poor countries, children do not always get this vaccine, and many still catch polio.

prejudice An unfair opinion of a person or group that is not based on fact. Some people are prejudiced against people who are disabled and doubt their abilities.

ramp A sloping floor or path that is used in place of—or in addition to—steps.

rickets A disease that mainly affects children. Rickets can occur if children do not eat enough foods containing vitamin D. The disease causes bones to become soft and deformed. Children can also be born with rickets if their mother did not eat the right foods while she was pregnant.

spina bifida A condition that occurs when a baby is growing inside its mother and parts of its spine do not line up properly. People with spina bifida have difficulty walking and might need braces, crutches, or a wheelchair to get around.

spinal cord A cord of nervous tissue that runs down a person's back. The brain passes nerve messages to the spinal cord. The spinal cord then sends the messages to all parts of the body, making muscles move. The spinal cord is protected by bones called vertebrae.

vaccine A liquid that is injected or swallowed to protect against a disease. The liquid contains a very weak form of the disease, which makes the body build up a resistance to that illness. If the person later comes into contact with the disease, she will not catch it.

vertebrae The small bones that run from the neck all the way down the back. They protect the sensitive spinal cord and support the rest of the body. These bones are called the backbone or the spinal column.

Useful addresses

For more information on physical disabilities, contact these organizations or visit their web sites.

Advocacy & Resource Center
327 N River Avenue
Suite 102
Holland, MI 49424
http://www.arc-resources.org/

American Association for the Advancement of Individuals with Disabilities
P.O. Box 4246
Clifton Park, NY 12065
http://www.aaaid.org/

American Association of People with Disabilities
1819 H Street NW
Suite 330
Washington, DC 20006
http://www.aapd.com/

American Disability Association
2201 6th Avenue South
Birmingham, AL 35233
http://www.adanet.org/

The Canadian Wheelchair Sports Association
1600 James Naismith Drive
Gloucester, ON K1B 5N4
http://indie.ca/cwsa/

National Center on Accessibility
5020 State Road 67 North
Martinsville, IN 46151
http://www.indiana.edu/~nca

National Council on Disability
1331 F Street NW
Suite 1050
Washington, DC 20004
http://www.ncd.gov/

Ontario March of Dimes
10 Overlea Blvd.
Toronto, ON M4H 1A4
http://www.omod.org/

Index